Going To My Ballet Class

Susan Kuklin

BRADBURY PRESS
New York

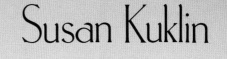

Bravo to all the children in Miss Dorothy's pre-ballet classes at the Joffrey Ballet School, but most especially those who participated in the making of this book: Bijoux Altramino, Mego Chen, Jami Noel English, Courtney Katon-Donegal, Edward Maas, Misha Morse, Sophia Ohara, David Rivera, Zane Selkirk, and Kamilah Warmington-Ewers. And thanks, too, to their parents.

The author would also like to thank:
Joffrey Ballet School, American Ballet Center   Edith D'Addario, Director, Joffrey Ballet School
Dorothy Lister   Dena Moss   Paul Lewis   Bill Lister   Trisha Noel and James English
Susan Preefer   Sharon Steinhoff   Julie Quan   Lynn Fischer

Copyright © 1989 by Susan Kuklin. All rights reserved. No part of this book may be reproduced or transmitted in any form or by any means, electronic or mechanical, including photocopying, recording, or by any information storage and retrieval system, without permission in writing from the Publisher.
Bradbury Press An Affiliate of Macmillan, Inc. 866 Third Avenue, New York, NY 10022
Collier Macmillan Canada, Inc. The text of this book is set in 16 point Bembo Medium.
Printed and bound in Japan
First American Edition   10 9 8 7 6 5 4 3 2 1

LIBRARY OF CONGRESS CATALOGING-IN-PUBLICATION DATA

Kuklin, Susan. Going to my ballet class/by Susan Kuklin. — 1st ed.   p.   cm.
Summary: A little girl describes, in text and illustrations, what she does in her ballet class.
Includes information on how to choose a ballet class for young children.
1. Ballet dancing—Juvenile literature.   [1. Ballet dancing.]   I. Title.
GV1787.5.K85 1989   792.8′2—dc19   88-37556   CIP   AC
ISBN 0-02-751235-5

For

Robert Joffrey

Every week my dad takes me to ballet class. As soon as we get to the school, he says, "Hurry and put on your leotard and tights, Jami, so that I can fix your hair." Miss Dorothy, my teacher, says our hair, just like our clothes, shouldn't get in the way of our dancing.

BEST ENTERTAINMENT IN NEW YORK

I have been in ballet class for one year. In the beginning, I had to work very hard to learn the steps, like the five arm and leg positions. Now some things are a little easier, but Miss Dorothy says even the best dancers must practice.

My classroom is very large. It has a mirror on one side and long poles, called barres, attached to the opposite wall.

I like to watch the older girls in the class before mine. Someday I hope I can dance like them.

Before we start our class, Paul, our piano player, shows us his music and tells us how to count to its beat. *One-and-two-and-three-and* . . .

When we dance, we have to know how much time we have to do each step. Counting the beats in the music helps.

The first thing we do in my class is form a big circle. We need lots of space to move, even for our warm-up exercises.

We sit in our circle, not talking, with straight backs, straight legs, and pointed toes. It sounds very easy, but it's hard to do all these things at the same time.

"Turn around, Jami," Miss Dorothy says, "and show the class a dancer's back. No lumps, please." Her assistant, Dena, tickles my back to remind me to sit up straight. "Now you look like dancers," Miss Dorothy says, and we're ready to begin.

We start with stretches for every part of our bodies. My teacher says these help make our muscles strong and flexible like rubber bands, not tight and stiff like sticks.

I like these best:

waist . . .

top of my legs . . .

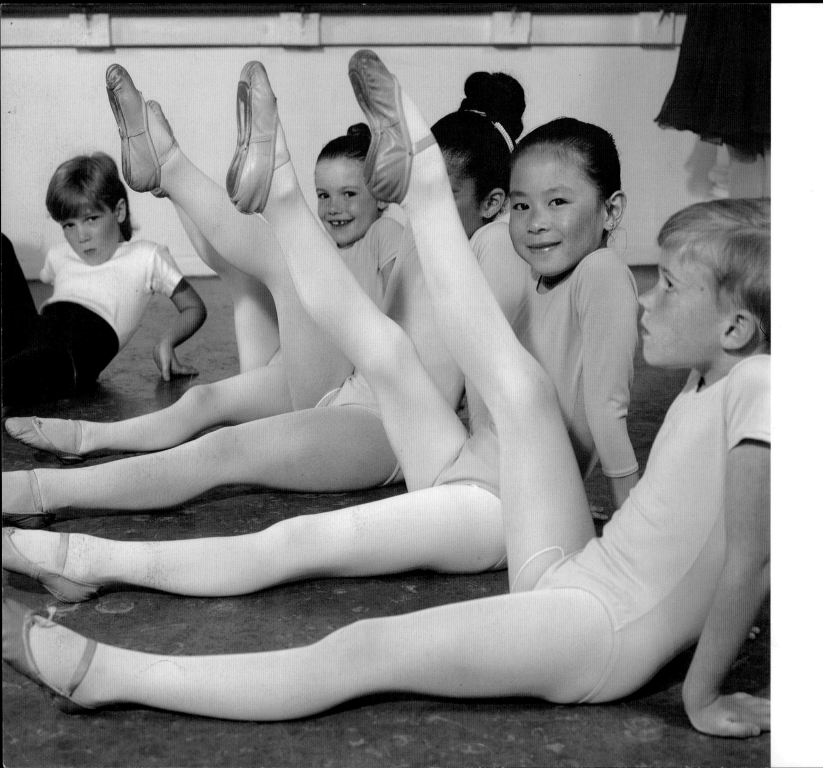

all of my legs

    . . . and back.

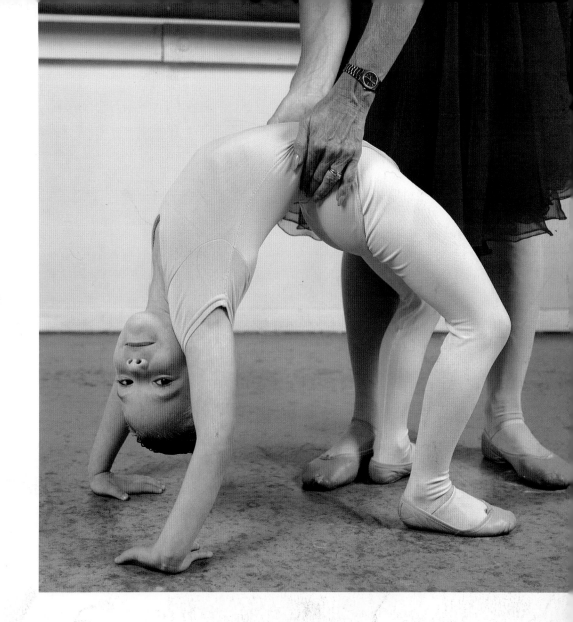

Stretching feels like a tiny pull. It doesn't hurt because
Miss Dorothy never lets us push too hard.

When we do our rocking and rolling exercise, I have to remember something else: my right side from my left. The music begins and Miss Dorothy calls out, "Right, left, right, left, right, left, ROLL."

We always get mixed up and bump into one another.

Then my teacher claps her hands
and says, "No good. Let's do it again."
When we're finished repeating
the exercise, Miss Dorothy cheers,
"That's it!" and we all go, *"Whew."*

Now that we're warmed up, we can stand in our circle and practice the ballet positions. Again, we need to keep our backs straight, tummies in, and legs straight. For each position we move only our arms, legs, and feet. My friends can do them well.

Kamilah in first . . .

Mego in second . . .

Edward in third . . .

Sophia in fourth . . .

Zane in fifth.

After all this standing still, Miss Dorothy says, "Now shake your hands . . . shake your right foot . . . your head. Shake everything!" Paul plays very fast, and we run all around the room.

Then my teacher claps. The music stops.
"Freeze in fifth!" she calls.

We have to think fast. I'm proud that
today I remember the right position.

When it's time to do cartwheels, we line up at the barre.
The hardest part is getting your legs over. It's scary being
upside down, but Miss Dorothy helps us if we need it, so we
always try and try again. Edward kicks up his legs and, for
the first time, flips all the way over! Wow!

After I take my turn, I say to Edward, "Do it again. Now that you've got it, you'll feel like you're a Ferris wheel."

My favorite part of class is when we get to watch ourselves in the mirror. Miss Dorothy puts us in a line. Then she says, "Glue your heels together in first position. Now pretend you have a glass of water on your heads and slowly plié."

"Plié" means to bend your knees in ballet language.

I try to make sure I don't spill the water. Miss Dorothy tells me, "You look so graceful, Jami, with your knees over your toes and your back straight. You are beginning to look like a dancer."

Next we get to put together a whole bunch of steps while we dance across the room. From a corner, we twirl around and around, moving our arms and legs in a special way, until we reach Dena in the opposite corner. It's easy to get dizzy with so much turning. Miss Dorothy tells us to keep our eyes on Dena and snap our heads toward her as we spin.

When it's my turn, I point my toe, count to the music, and snap my head. Once I reach Dena, we hold hands and I make an L with my arms.

Just before class is over, we practice our leaps. This is my
second favorite part. One at a time we race to Miss Dorothy
and leap over a long stick, keeping our legs straight. The
music goes fast and so do we.

I take a chance and try to jump really high because I don't
want to hit that stick.

Zane does it best.
She can really fly!

Now we're at the end. With ballet walking steps—toe, heel, toe, heel—I go to Miss Dorothy. We bow to each other.

Ballet class makes me feel strong and smart and grown-up. But most of all, it makes me want to keep dancing.

HOW TO CHOOSE A BALLET CLASS

The two most important aspects of a ballet class for young children are, first, whether it is safe, and second, whether it is fun. A parent can judge these features by observing a class before enrolling his or her child. Classes should not be so crowded that personal attention cannot be given to each child. The program, very simple at first, should be working toward clearly defined goals.

Very young dancers should not be pushed to do difficult routines which demand more than they are physically and emotionally ready for. Technique, such as the "turn out," should not be taught until the child is at least eight years old, because it puts too much physical stress on the body. Although ballet is based upon discipline, the discipline must be appropriate for the age of the child. The ideal class is one that is run in an orderly fashion but that includes a chance for the children to relax and let loose. The joy of dance cannot get forgotten.

Dorothy Lister, the teacher in this book, heads the children's division of the Joffrey Ballet School. Because so many young children wanted to take dance, she designed a pre-ballet curriculum that strengthens the back, protects the feet, and introduces the beginning *form* of ballet technique.

Since most youngsters do not have the muscle power to stand for long periods, much of class is spent sitting on the floor in a circle. "Until they can hold their backs in a nice and straight sitting position, they will be unable to do ballet standing up," Lister says. The teacher and her assistant are often in the circle with the class.

When this particular pre-ballet class first began, some of the children took one look at the studio and the teacher and, in Miss Dorothy's words, "turned pea green." Few knew right from left — which foot was which. They needed to be trained, but in an interesting way so that they would have fun and want to come back. Lister started off very easy. As the class progressed, students learned the five positions, the difference between a bent leg and a straight leg and a bent foot and a straight foot, to count to the music, to move right to left without too much hesitation, and to coordinate their arms with their bodies.

The children in Lister's pre-ballet classes do not learn the actual ballet steps; rather, they learn the form that will lead to the steps. For example, after Jami twirls across the room to Dena, she forms an L shape with her arms. That's the start of an arabesque. Although Lister does not refer to the arabesque in these classes, once her students begin their formal ballet training, they will have already learned the beginnings of an arabesque.

As the year proceeded, the children began to accomplish various routines. They felt good about themselves, stronger and more secure, when they saw they were capable of performing Miss Dorothy's directives. With the improvement, Lister edged them into more complex routines.

A ballet school's reputation can be checked through one of the many dance teachers' associations, such as Dance Masters of America (Wauchula, Florida [813] 773-2417) and Dance Educators of America (Oceanside, New York [516] 766-6615); local universities or colleges that have dance departments; or periodicals such as *Dance Magazine*. Instructors who were formerly professional dancers are more likely to have extensive training and performing experience.